Contents

CONTENTS

TALK LESS
—AND—
SAY MORE

Vermont Proverbs

Wolfgang Mieder

Woodcuts by Mary Azarian

Cathy —

Always keep Vermont
in your heart !

11/17/86 Wolfgang Mieder

The New England Press
Shelburne, Vermont

ISBN 0-933050-42-9
Library of Congress Catalog Card Number: 86-50974
First Edition

Designed by Andrea Gray
Printed in the United States of America
For additional copies of this book or for a catalog
of our other New England titles, please write:

The New England Press
P.O. Box 575
Shelburne, VT 05482

Introduction

In his long epic poem *The People, Yes* (1930), Carl Sandburg, by assembling hundreds of examples of traditional speech patterns, depicted the various ethnic groups and nationalities which make up the melting pot of the United States. He knew that the language of the common people with its idioms, slang, proverbial expressions, and proverbs could best describe what these heterogeneous people are all about:

> The people is Everyman, everybody.
> Everybody is you and me and
> all others.
> What everybody says is what we
> all say.
> And what is it we all say?

The answer to this question is in part proverbs, for they express concisely apparent truths that have currency among the people of a nation or a region at any given time. These proverbs might not be of the highest philosophical value, but they contain certain basic truths about everyday existence. As formulaic and traditional expressions of wisdom, proverbs have played a significant role in human communication for centuries, and there is no doubt that they are of continued importance as ready-made expressions of general experiences.

Proverbs have been defined in various ways, and erudite paremiologists (proverb scholars) include such characteristics as structure, metaphor, form, style, variation, meaning, and context. Leaving such details to scholars for a moment, suffice it to say that a proverb is still quite appropriately defined by Lord John Russell's proverbial maxim, "a proverb is the wit of one and the wisdom of many" (ca. 1850). This means that every proverb was originally coined by an individual, and if its language and content merited repetition it was adopted by others until it gained a general acceptance in a family, a village, a city, a county, a state, a country, or eventually the world. There are even proverbs about proverbs which help to clarify what a proverb is; for example, "Proverbs are the coins of people," "Proverbs are the children of experience," or "Proverbs are the wisdom of ages." Someone has called them, rather poetically, "monumenta humana," but I propose as a more concrete definition—a composite of dozens of such definitions from various cultures and times —the following formulation: A proverb is a short, generally known sentence that expresses common, traditional, and often didactic views in a metaphorical and fixed form which is easily remembered and repeated.

The fact that proverbs are complete sentences, albeit with poetic ellipses, differentiates them from such proverbial expressions as "To throw the baby out with the bathwater" or proverbial comparisons such as "Poor as a church mouse." Such formulaic expressions need to be incorporated into the flow of speech just as single words or idioms are, while the proverb functions as a self-contained and complete thought. Proverbial expressions could be looked at as the metaphorical mortar of everyday communication, while proverbs represent the solid building blocks. Proverbs also always contain some grain of truth or wisdom, while proverbial expressions primarily add colorful flavor to our language. Thus, if Robert Frost says "Good fences make good neighbors," he is clearly citing a proverb, one which has been traced back to 1640 in the variant form, "A good fence helpeth to keepe peace betweene neighbours."

This shows, of course, that this particular proverb was most likely not coined in Vermont but maybe in Massachusetts or more probably in England. Discovering the origin of each proverb is an extremely complicated matter that involves detailed historical and comparative research. Many proverbs such as "One hand washes the other" or "Time flies" appear in the earliest proverb collections of antiquity. They have been translated into many languages and have almost worldwide currency. Clearly they are also in use in the United States and thus in Vermont. Such international proverbs can therefore be included in national or regional proverb collections if one keeps in mind that their inclusion signifies the currency of the proverb in that area but not necessarily its actual origin there. A collection of "American Proverbs," for example, will contain dozens of texts which are in fact British or even translations into English from much earlier classical sources. The key issue, however, is that they are being used in the United States as if they were "American."

A similar problem arises in regional proverb collections such as this one. I have tried to exclude proverbs which are standard in all parts of the United States. This means that proverbs like "Don't look a gift horse in the mouth," "Early to bed and early to rise, makes a man healthy, wealthy, and wise," or

"A penny saved is a penny earned" are definitely not included. Some proverbs in our small collection like "Vermont has only two seasons—winter and the Fourth of July" or "It's time to plant corn when the icicles fall off the ledge on Snake Mountain" are obviously truly Vermont proverbs, but how about such proverbs as "Sap runs best after a sharp frost," "The world is your cow, but you have to do the milking," or "Every cider apple has a worm"? They sound like they originated in Vermont, but why not in New Hampshire or New York? Only through painstaking research of each individual proverb might the actual origin come to light, but for many such texts the proof of a Vermont source would be impossible. What is of importance is that many of the proverbs in the present collection probably originated among Vermonters and that the rest are without doubt current in the state of Vermont. Heeding these points, we can legitimately call the present collection "Vermont Proverbs."

One additional caveat should be mentioned. There is a certain amount of danger connected with deducing national or regional characteristics from proverbs. Obviously the almost five hundred proverbs assembled here do not describe the "typical" Vermonter, if there is in fact such a person. However, proverbs do reflect to a certain degree the world view of their users, and with caution one could perhaps say that this collection of folk wisdom current in Vermont reflects the stereotypic view of Vermonters. Many proverbs deal with cows, maple sugaring, independence, thriftiness, and taciturnity, which all seem to be part of the Vermont scene and psyche. Others express a good dose of the dry humor which Vermonters are supposedly famous for. Above all, the proverbs reflect in concise and picturesque language a way of life which appeals to real Vermonters and so-called "flatlanders" alike. There are lucid gems of wisdom in this little florilegium of Vermont proverbs which will be entertaining and edifying at the same time. The value of the Vermont folk wisdom is still high, so let us, in agreement with Carl Sandburg's positive esteem for proverbs, "behold the proverbs of a people, a nation" —in this case picturesque Vermont proverbs.

This collection of proverbs from Vermont is based on oral and literary sources. The regional literature of such Vermont authors as Rowland E. Robinson, John Godfrey Saxe, Dorothy Canfield Fisher, Walter Hard, and Allen R. Foley provided numerous texts. I am also indebted to the scholarly writings of two former University of Vermont professors, Muriel Hughes and Leon Dean, who explored Vermont folklore and proverbs before me. The many issues of Vermont's two folklore journals, *The Potash Kettle* and *Green Mountain Whittlin's,* yielded many additional proverbs. Many other sources on various aspects of Vermont life were consulted, but a large number of the proverbs were collected in oral use during the past fifteen years. Their oral currency and their appearance in the written media clearly indicate that these texts can be considered proverbs from Vermont. The proverbs which appear in this small collection represent those texts of my larger archive which distinguish themselves in particular due to their metaphorical language and regional flavor. They are divided into twenty-one general sections which reflect normal aspects of life. But see for yourself what Vermonters think and say about life in this wonderful part of the world called Vermont.

ADVICE
AND
KNOWLEDGE

Stretch your arm no longer than
your sleeve will reach.

There is a difference knowing how to
think and what to think.

Do not whistle until you're
out of the woods.

A handsaw is a good thing, but not
to shave with.

A new broom sweeps clean, but the
old one finds the corners.

The still pig eats the swill.

If you believe all you hear, you can
eat all you see.

Never ride a free horse to death.

An empty sack can't stand.

A woodpecker never touches
a healthy tree.

It's a queer world and few
get out alive.

Unless the kettle boiling be, filling
the pot spoils the tea.

Never throw away food that will make
a pig open his mouth.

Hope is a good breakfast but
a bad supper.

Every sow has to bury her own nose
in the swill.

It takes more than one well to
make a river.

It's hard paying for a dead horse.

It is a lean cow that gives the milk.

MONEY
AND
THRIFTINESS

Money makes the mare go—but not
the nightmare.

At a good bargain pause awhile.

If you're giving away an old coat,
don't cut off the buttons.

Dirty hands make clean money.

Debt is the worst kind of poverty.

You get what you pay for.

A small home is better than
a large mortgage.

Save up your money, pile up your
rocks, and you'll always have tobacco
in the old tobacco box.

If you don't do any more than you are
paid for, you won't get paid for any
more than you do.

What costs, counts.

It is better to be neat and tidy than
to be tight and needy.

The cobbler's child is always barefoot.

A pig on credit makes a good winter
and a bad spring.

A new day, a new dollar.

An empty purse puts wrinkles
in the face.

Keep a thing seven years and it will
sort of do.

Economy is the poor man's bank.

There's no disgrace in poverty, but
it's damned inconvenient.

Money won't buy happiness, but it's
nice to choose your way
to be unhappy.

Charity begins at home and usually
stays there.

When in doubt, do without.

One pair of good soles is worth two
pairs of upper leather.

He who buys what he does not need
will sometimes need what
he cannot buy.

Take care of the dimes and the dollars
will take care of themselves.

FRIENDS
AND
ACQUAINTANCES

You have to hoe a row of corn with a man
to know him.

Love thy neighbor
as thyself—but no more.

Friendship can't stand on one leg long.

Pleasure makes us acquainted with each
other, but it takes trials and grief
to make us know each other.

In a horse trade you got to know either
the horse or the man.

All are not saints that go to church.

You have to summer and winter
together before you know
each other.

Patch by patch is neighborly, but patch
on patch is beggarly.

A constant guest is never welcome.

He who plants trees loves others
besides himself.

The latchstring is always out
for a friend.

False friends are worse than
open enemies.

A dog is a man's best friend, but a
good cow is more help at the table.

Love your neighbor, yet don't pull
down the hedge.

Wise distrust is the parent of security.

Eat a peck of salt with a man before
you trust him.

Good fences make good neighbors.

CHANCE
AND
OPPORTUNITIES

The early robin looks for worms
behind the early plow.

Gold is where you find it.

Mend the first break, kill the first
snake, and conquer everything
you undertake.

The time to pick berries is when
they're ripe.

Reach for the high apples first; you
can get the low ones any time.

A crooked road won't get you far.

Time to catch bears is when
they are out.

Better be ready and not go than to go
and not be ready.

Take what you get and be
thankful for that.

Milk the cow which is near.

If you must kick, kick towards the goal.

There's no use keeping a dog
and barking yourself.

You can sheer a sheep many times but
you can skin him only once.

Measure your cloth ten times; you can
cut but once.

Don't saw off the branch you
are sitting on.

You can't keep trouble from coming,
but you don't have to give it a
chair to sit on.

A beaten road is the safest.

Sing before breakfast, cry
before evening.

Better three hours too soon than one
minute too late.

Every cow needs a tail in fly time.

Take the good and leave the rest.

A little spark may kindle a great fire.

When you buy the land, you buy the
stones; when you buy the meat, you
buy the bones.

If the dog hadn't stopped to sniff the
tree, he would have caught the fox.

FREEDOM
—— AND ——
INDEPENDENCE

A bird in a cage will fly away.

Every tub must sit on its own bottom.

He who has sense has strength.

You can't hang a man for an idea.

A little leeway gives a little freeway.

Anything worth having is worth
fighting for.

He governs best who governs least.

All men are born free and eager.

Happiness is a horse you
cannot harness.

He that is bound must obey.

Give neither salt nor counsel until
asked for it.

Thoughts are free from toll.

He sees best who sees the consequences.

Independence is better than riches.

APPEARANCES
AND
DECEPTIONS

The grass always looks greener in the
other fellow's yard.

One swallow doesn't make a summer.

Self-praise doesn't go a great ways.

You can't judge a man by his overcoat.

Wrinkles and patches don't show on
a trotting horse.

You can't judge others by your self.

Half the dwellers in glass houses don't
seem to know it.

You can never tell the depth of the
well from the length of the handle
on the pump.

Hasty glory goes out in a snuff.

You can't always tell by the looks of
a toad how far he can jump.

Painted flowers have no scent.

Better be dead than out of fashion.

It isn't always the bell cow that gives
the most milk.

A long face shortens your following.

You can't judge a horse by its harness.

Every cook praises his own broth.

You can't judge a book by its binding.

Beauty does not make the pot boil.

An empty wagon rumbles loud.

A teaspoon of sugar draws more flies
than a gallon of vinegar.

Handsome apples are sometimes sour.

Every horse thinks his own pack
the heaviest.

Dirt is dirtiest upon the fairest spot.

The fountain is clearest at its source.

Some people will cry poor on
a full stomach.

He that goes softly, goes safely.

Cows prefer the grass on the other
side of the fence.

You won't hurt a smile by cracking it.

The empty bowl makes the most noise.

A good gaper makes several more.

Every man thinks his own geese swans.

You can't judge a cow by her looks.

ANCESTRY
AND
HERITAGE

Ancestors are a poor excuse for not
amounting to a hill of beans.

A son should begin where his
father left off.

No man dies without an heir.

It's a dirty bird that fouls his own nest.

A good name is better than gold.

Unworthy offspring brag the most about
their worthy descendants.

A good cow may have a bad calf.

Blood is thicker than water if it
is worth anything.

An apple never falls far from the tree.

There is enough underbrush in every
family to burn out all the good wood.

STRENGTH
AND
PERSEVERANCE

The squeaking hinge gets the most oil.

The best things are hard to come by.

What you lose in the dance, you make
up in the turnabout.

Constant dripping wears away
the hardest stone.

A creaking gate never breaks.

Little strokes fell great oaks.

If you want to get to the top of the
hill, you must go up it.

A tree falls not at the first stroke.

A squealing pig gets fed.

A creaking door hangs long
on the hinges.

Don't swallow the cow and worry
with the tail.

Slow but sure wins the race.

Grain by grain the hen fills her belly.

It's the squeaking axle that
gets the grease.

Behind the clouds the sun
is still shining.

Step by step the ladder is climbed.

Keep straight and you'll never get into
trouble or grow round-shouldered.

What is hard to bear is
sweet to remember.

The constant creeping of ants will
wear away the stone.

ILLS
AND
DISAPPOINTMENTS

Every cider apple has a worm.

Sometimes the cheese is blamed when
the fault is in the ventilation.

There's always one fool fox
in every litter.

One scabbed sheep will infect
a whole flock.

Little minds run in the same ditch.

There is small choice in rotten apples.

Good riddance to bad rubbish.

It is impossible to spoil what
never was good.

Every cask smells of the wine
it contains.

Some people aren't fit to root
with a pig.

A rotten apple spoils its companion.

There's always something to keep
the bunny's tail short.

It makes a difference whose cow
is in the well.

From a great supper comes a great pain.

You never miss the water till
the well runs dry.

WORK
── AND ──
LAZINESS

The world is your cow, but you have to do the milking.

It's a poor man that doesn't work hard enough to wet the back of his shirt.

Business neglected is business lost.

Contrivance is as good as hard work.

When men are rightly occupied, their amusement grows out of their work.

It's better to wear out than to rust out.

Diligence is the mother of good fortune.

Laziness and poverty go hand in hand.

The more you do, the more you may and the less you're thanked for it.

If you don't use your head, you will have to use your feet.

Hard work never hurt anybody.

Lazy folks work the best when the sun is in the west.

A good night's rest gives a good feeling day.

A lazy carpenter fights with his tools.

If you can't help, don't hinder.

Wishing isn't doing.

A sitting hen never grows fat.

It's a bad workman that loses his tools.

An hour before sunrise is worth two thereafter.

The sleepy fox catches no chickens.

They must hunger in frost that will
not work in heat.

Don't send a boy on a man's errand.

Industry brings plenty.

Some are always busy but never
do a thing.

A used key is always bright.

It takes a crank to start the wheel.

By doing nothing we learn to do ill.

Laziness travels so slowly that poverty
soon overtakes it.

All play and no work makes Jack
a mere toy.

Don't wait till you're tired before
taking a rest.

Between ten and two will tell
what the day will do.

Those who make no mistakes seldom
do anything at all.

A task well begun is half done.

A work ill done must be done twice.

How beautiful it is to do nothing
and then rest afterwards.

It's nice to sit and think but sometimes
it's nicer just to sit.

If you haven't enough to do, start
cleaning your own backyard.

Never show a fool a job half done.

Sow an act, reap a habit.

The lazy dog leans to the wall to bark.

WISHES
AND
IMPOSSIBILITIES

You can't make a whistle out of
a pig's tail.

Wishes can't fill a sack.

You can't get wool off a frog.

Fly from pleasure that will
bite tomorrow.

You can't expect anything from a pig
but a grunt.

It isn't the whistle that pulls the train.

You can't swing a cat by a bull's tail.

It's a poor foot that can't shape
its own stocking.

You can't mow hay where the
grass doesn't grow.

Wishes and wailings mend nothing.

It's a poor crust that can't grease
its own plate.

You can't make a crooked stick
lay straight.

An old tree cannot be transplanted.

You can't put a quart in a pint basin.

The steam that toots a whistle will
never turn a wheel.

You can't build a house from
the top down.

It's a poor back that can't press
its own shirt.

Wishes won't do dishes.

You can't sell the cow and have
the milk too.

SPEECH
AND
SILENCE

Talk less and say more.

Three can keep a secret if two
of them are dead.

Few words are best.

Saying and doing are two things.

The belly is not filled with fair words.

Anything worth making is worth saying.

Soft words break no bones.

Say nothing and saw wood.

He can't speak well who always talks.

A story without an author is not
worth listening to.

Deeds are fruits, words are but leaves.

What soberness conceals,
drunkenness reveals.

If you have to whisper it,
better not say it.

If you can't say good things of others,
keep your mouth shut.

He who thinks by the inch and talks by
the yard gets moved by the foot.

A person's speech reveals the soul.

Silence is prudence.

Nobody ever repented holding
his tongue.

A kind word never broke a tooth.

Be silent or speak something
worth hearing.

Words are but wind, but seeing
is believing.

What you don't say won't ever
hurt you.

Where there is whispering,
there is lying.

Never speak loudly to one another
unless the house is on fire.

A dead dog tells no tales.

Turn your tongue seven times
before speaking.

Never cackle unless you lay.

Your word is your gold.

The least said the soonest mended.

Speech is silver and silence is golden.

A good word now is worth ten
on a headstone.

RESIGNATION
AND
CONSOLATION

Dunghills rise and castles fall.

Many have by far too much,
but nobody enough.

Things at the worst will
sometimes mend.

Live and learn and die fools at last.

No matter how tough the roast beef is,
you can always cut the gravy
with your knife.

It is better to smoke here than
in the hereafter.

We shall all be alike in our graves.

Time cuts down all, both
great and small.

The smaller the peas the more to a pod.

You'll never go hungry with salt
pork and potatoes.

Live while you live and then die
and be done with it.

What can't be cured must be endured.

Pity is a poor plaster.

So goes Monday, so goes all the week.

Hope well and have well.

You'll catch your death just as sure
as you live.

Every dog has his day and the cats
their nights.

Don't cry over spilt milk; there's
enough water in it already.

Leaves have their time to fall.

QUARRELS
AND
DISAGREEMENTS

Save your chips for kindling, not for
wear on your shoulders.

Toes that are tender will
be stepped upon.

He that handles a nettle tenderly
is soonest stung.

You can't play with fire without
burning your fingers.

Give a calf enough rope and it
will hang itself.

Mud thrown is ground lost.

No roof can cover two families.

When you argue with a fool,
that makes two.

The absent person is always at fault.

Laws are like cobwebs where the small
flies are caught and the big ones
break through.

Follow your bad instincts, and you will
perish a sinner.

Quarrelsome dogs come limping home.

The credit got by a lie lasts only until
the truth comes out.

Sit between two stools and you'll
reach the floor.

Some people hang out more
than they wash.

Anger and pride are both unwise.

There's many a chill, but few are frozen.

Sometimes a burden is fitted to the back,
but mostly it's ready made.

Don't be dipping your lip in
another's porridge.

Correct in yourself what you
blame in others.

No offense being meant, none
should be took.

There's nothing to be gained by
airing dirty linen.

When the bow is too much bent,
it breaks.

It doesn't pay to fight a skunk, because
if you win, you lose.

It makes a difference whose ox is gored.

Cursed cows have short horns.

The law catches flies but lets
hornets go free.

There is more than one way to kill a
cat besides soaking him in butter.

No one ever forgets where he
buried the hatchet.

YOUTH
AND
AGE

Give a pig when it grunts and a child
when it cries, and you will have
a fine pig and a bad child.

As the twig is bent, the tree is inclined.

Little pitchers have big ears.

You will follow the path in old age
that you made for yourself
in your youth.

There's less pain to learn in youth
than to be ignorant in age.

An old horse knows its way home.

You may break a colt, but not
an old horse.

A young twig is easier twisted
than an old tree.

To govern a child is to govern
yourself first.

Young people don't know what age is
and old people forget what youth was.

Time is the rider that breaks youth.

Death keeps no calendar.

Never was an old shoe but had an old
stocking to match it.

A tree falls in the direction
that it leans.

He who runs in youth may lie
down in age.

You will never learn younger.

Age listens to the voice of experience.

You can't put an old head
on young shoulders.

WIVES
AND
WOMEN

Choose a wife rather by your ear
than your eye.

Better an old man's darling than
a young man's slave.

A woman can throw out more with a
spoon than a man can bring home
with a shovel.

An old maid doesn't know anything
but what she imagines.

Never run after a woman. They are like
streetcars. Stand still, for another
one will come along soon.

Silks and satins put out
the kitchen fire.

A woman's tongue is sharper than
a double-edged sword.

It's better to live on the top of the
house than with a contentious woman.

The best time to select a wife is
in the morning.

You know a good housekeeper
by her windows.

Better a fortune in a wife than
with a wife.

Gold is tested with fire, a woman with
gold, and a man with woman.

Kissing a girl because she is willing
is like scratching a place that
doesn't itch.

Whistling girls and jumping sheep
always come to the top of the heap.

The best furniture in a house is
a virtuous woman.

Dimple outside, devil inside.

A barn, a fence, and a woman
always need mending.

A good wife and health is a man's
best wealth.

Generally speaking, woman is
generally speaking.

MEN
AND
MANLINESS

Men and melons are hard to know.

Where the cobwebs grow,
the beaux don't go.

A man may kiss his cow.

Men aren't worth the salt of a
woman's tears.

Any man can strut; the pompous man
can strut standing still.

A poor man finds fault with his tools.

The bigger the man, the bigger the fall.

A man is as old as he feels, and a
woman is as old as she looks.

An old bachelor is half a
pair of scissors.

A young man idle and an old man needy.

Wood warms a man twice.

A fool never makes a good husband.

Rich men's tables have few crumbs.

A man does not look behind the door
unless he has stood there himself.

Every man has his price.

A poor man always keeps a dog, and a
very poor man keeps two.

A reformed rake makes the
best husband.

A quarrelsome man has no
good neighbors.

Wise men are like timber trees in a
hedge: here and there one.

LOVE
AND
MARRIAGE

It is well to be off with the old love
before you are on with the new.

A warm-back husband and a cold-foot
wife should easily lead a compatible life.

A kiss without whiskers is like an
egg without salt.

She who is a beauty is half married.

There's no Jack without a Jill; if one
won't, another will.

A man that cheats his wife may
cheat many others.

Love and a cough cannot be hidden.

It is better to be half-hanged
than ill wed.

Marry your sons when you will, your
daughters when you can.

When poverty comes in at the door, love
flies out at the window.

There's no help for misfortune but
to marry again.

A deaf husband and a blind wife are
always a happy couple.

There may be snow on the roof but
there's fire in the cellar.

An old man marrying a young girl is
like buying a book for someone
else to read.

Always to court and never to wed is
the happiest life that ever was led.

It's a lonesome washing when there's
not a man's shirt in it.

PLANTING
AND
HARVESTING

It's a rare farm that has no bad ground.

A small seed sometimes produces
a large tree.

It's time to plant corn when the icicles
fall off the ledge on Snake Mountain.

Sow peas and beans in the wane
of the moon.

If the corn has thick husks, there will
be a hard winter.

Town Meeting is time to put in
the potatoes.

Plant your corn when the leaves of the
oak tree are the size of a mouse's ear.

When you see the swallows, it is time
to sow oats.

Plant cucumbers the first Sunday in
June before sunrise.

It's time to plant corn when
the toads trill.

He that observes the wind and the rain
shall not reap.

Sow dry and set wet.

Snowy winter, plentiful harvest.

Time to plant beans is when it is hot
enough nights so Hannah sleeps
without a sheet on her.

If the farmer fails all will starve.

Your corn will never grow until you lie
naked at night.

Plow deep while others sleep and you
shall have corn to sell and keep.

SAP
AND
SUGARING

A gallon of syrup is worth
one day's labor.

When the sun is bright on the snow and
warm on your back, the sap will
be running.

The more sap the more sugar.

When the buds start on the trees, it is
time to gather the buckets.

The lower you tap the more the sap.

Warm days, cold nights, make
sap run right.

Sap runs best after a sharp frost.

The older the tree the sweeter the sap.

Sap runs better by day than by night.

When the moon of April glows the
maple sap flows.

A tree will run the most sap on the
side where it has the coarsest bark.

Tap when you can get sap
in the spout.

If the trees go into winter with wet
feet, there will be a good sap-season.

When the snow-fleas start flying, it is
time to tap the maple trees.

Trees by a brook or spring run much sap.

You boil at least thirty-two gallons of
sap to make each gallon of syrup.

Sap run during the daytime is sweeter
than that run at night.

When the wind is in the west the sap
runs the best.

The first run of sap is the sweetest.

Gather often, boil at once.

The higher you tap the
sweeter the sap.

When the good Lord says that the sap
will run it doesn't make any difference
whether it is twelve o'clock at night or
eight o'clock in the morning.

Sap early in the season and late in the
season is the sweetest.

The better the sap season the
better the sugar.

Sap runs before a rain and after a snow.

Trees differ as much for sugar as cows
differ for butter.

Sugaring is a lot like a poker game:
you're in it before you know it.

A sap-run is the sweet good-bye
of winter.

The true Vermonter never loses his taste
for the sweet of the maple.

WEATHER
AND
SEASONS

If you don't like the weather,
wait a minute.

Fog goes up the mountain a hoppin',
rain comes down a droppin'.

If the cat should sneeze it will
rain or freeze.

It won't be warm till the snow gets off
the mountain, and the snow won't get off
the mountain till it gets warm.

The swallows fly high, no rain in the
sky; swallows skim the hay, rain
the next day.

Vermont has nine months of winter and three months of damned poor sledding.

Milk makes cream most freely with a north wind.

Winter's fog will freeze a dog.

A full moon on Christmas means a poor hay crop.

The frost hurts no weeds.

A sunshiny shower won't last half an hour.

It takes more than one robin to make a summer.

A late snowstorm is a poor man's fertilizer.

Clear moon, frost soon.

The more rain the more rest, dry weather is not always the best.

Take off your flannels before the first of May and you'll have a doctor's bill to pay.

Snow on Mount Mansfield and in six
weeks the valley will be white.

A cold wet May fills the barn
full of hay.

March rains serve only to fill ditches.

Snow takes the place of manure.

Rain before seven, dry before eleven.

No warm weather until the snow comes
and goes three times.

If March comes in like a lion, it's more
than likely to go out like the devil.

Fog on the hills, more water
for the mills.

A late fall means a hard winter.

If cows lie down before noon it
will rain soon.

Button to the chin till May be in.

Vermont has only two seasons—
winter and the Fourth of July.